OXFORD
UNIVERSITY PRESS

Great Clarendon Street, Oxford OX2 6DP

Oxford is a registered trade mark of Oxford
University Press in the UK and in certain other countries

Series created by Ruth Miskin
Text by Ruth Miskin and Mitch Cronick
Illustrations by Tim Archbold

ISBN 978 0198386704

10 9 8 7 6 5 4 3 2 1
Printed in China by Imago

Paper used in the production of this book is a natural, recyclable product
made from wood grown in sustainable forests. The manufacturing process
conforms to the environmental regulations of the country of origin.

www.oxfordprimary.co.uk

Handbook

Help your child to read with phonics

Ruth Miskin
and
Mitch Cronick

OXFORD

UNIVERSITY PRESS

Contents

Dear Parent/Guardian

While I was a headteacher in London I began to devise a programme that would get all children to read and write quickly and easily. The programme has now been widely used tested and developed and the result is *Read Write Inc. Phonics*.

Following the huge success of *Read Write Inc. Phonics* in schools, and many parental requests, I have created books and flashcards for use at home.

At the core of *Read Write Inc. Phonics* is the systematic teaching of all the 44 common sounds in the English language. Children are taught to read and say the sounds and to put them together, to 'sound-blend' them, into words for reading.

First you need to help your child learn the sounds on the Flashcards. Once your child has done this, read the books for about twenty minutes at least five times a week; little and often is far more effective than an hour every now and again.

If you follow the step-by-step advice given in this Handbook and ensure your child does the activities before and after reading each story, you will be giving your child the best possible support. Day by day, you will see your child's confidence grow — and there are few things more rewarding than seeing your child learn to read.

Best wishes,

Ruth Mishn

Read Write Inc. Phonics Materials

The *Read Write Inc. Phonics* series contains all you need to get your child reading at home.

Handbook

This Handbook will give you detailed, easy-to-follow advice on using the Flashcards and Storybooks so that you can support your child at every stage.

At first there may seem to be a lot of activities to get through, but they are *quick* to do and have proven to be highly effective in helping children learn to read. When your child has done the activities once, it's easy to remember what to do the next time and there are simplified notes in the Storybooks.

Don't be tempted just to read the stories to your child and then ask him or her to read them to you. If you do this, your child will probably just remember the words, have no real practice in reading and be unable to read the words without the support of the pictures.

Flashcards

Before your child can start to read, he or she needs to learn to:

⭐ say the sound that is represented by each letter or group of letters

⭐ 'sound out' the word, e.g. *c-a-t, sh-o-p, s-t-r-ee-t.*

In *Read Write Inc. Phonics* the individual sounds are called 'Speed sounds' – because we want your child to read them effortlessly. The Flashcards contain all the Speed sounds your child needs to learn to enable him or her to read the Storybooks.

However, knowing letters and their corresponding sounds is not enough to get a child reading. Your child needs to learn how to sound out the letters in a word *and* how to blend them together to read it. This is called 'sound-blending'.

The Flashcards have ten Instruction cards with fun activities for practising sound-blending with your child.

Storybooks

When your child can sound-blend the Speed sounds from the Flashcards he or she can then progress to reading the Storybooks.

These have lively, rhyming stories that are fun to read. They enable your child to practise reading the sounds already learnt as they contain words made up of the Speed sounds on the Flashcards. So they are carefully matched to your child's reading level.

Level 1 books are the simplest and each one contains four short rhyming stories. They will help your child to practise:

- ⭐ sound-blending to make words
- ⭐ reading short, simple words
- ⭐ reading simple sentences.

Your child could read one of these stories a night.

Level 2 books each contain two longer stories with more challenging words to read. They will help to practise:

- ⭐ blending letter sounds to make words
- ⭐ reading simple sentences
- ⭐ reading short, rhyming stories.

Level 3 books each contain one long story which will develop your child's reading stamina. They will help to practise:

⭐ reading longer sentences

⭐ reading extended stories.

If your child is properly prepared for reading the words in the stories, he or she will be more likely to read the stories successfully and enjoy them. Therefore, the Storybooks contain activities to ensure your child is ready to read and activities to reinforce what has been read.

The notes on pages 14–19 explain how to do each activity, step-by-step, and why each one is important.

Remember, all children need encouragement when learning to read, so do praise your child's efforts as he or she works to complete each step.

Using the Flashcards

Before your child starts to read the Storybooks, he or she should learn to read the Speed sounds on the Flashcards and then how to sound-blend them into words, e.g. *c-a-t* → *cat*.

Use the Flashcards to teach your child the Speed sounds. These are the letter sounds, *not* the letter names, so *m* as in *mat* not *em*, and *s* as in *sun* not *es*.

For each Speed sound there is a Flashcard with a simple picture prompt on one side and the letter or letters that represent that sound on the other. There is also a card with two pictures of things that contain that sound.

Using the activities on the Instruction flashcards, teach your child two sounds each day. Always review the sounds already learnt, as a reminder.

Don't let your child become too reliant on using the picture prompt to remember the sound. Once he or she knows a sound without referring to the picture, don't show the picture prompt again.

Guidance on how to write the letters correctly is given on page 22.

Say: c-c-c-caterpillar
(Bouncy sound)

The Speed sounds have been divided into small groups. Once your child has learnt all the sounds in a group he or she can progress to sound-blending that group of Speed sounds into words. (See below.) Then your child can learn the next group of Speed sounds, how to sound-blend them, and so on, until he or she is confident with all the groups. At this point your child will be ready to read the Storybooks.

Teach your child the Speed sounds in this order:

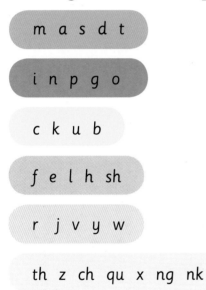

m a s d t

i n p g o

c k u b

f e l h sh

r j v y w

th z ch qu x ng nk

The colour strip at the top of each Flashcard shows the group it belongs to. Note that sometimes one sound is represented by more than one letter: *sh* as in *sh-i-p*, *th* as in *th-i-n*, *ch* as in *ch-a-t*, *qu* as in *qu-i-t* and *ng* as in *s-i-ng*. These letters should be pronounced as one sound. The letters *nk* are also taught as one sound.

Bouncy and stretchy sounds

On the Flashcards it states whether the Speed sound is 'stretchy' or 'bouncy'. It will help your child remember the sounds if you bounce the bouncy sounds in a short, sharp way with a gap in between, e.g. *d-d-d-dinosaur*, and stretch the stretchy sounds in one continuous sound, e.g. *mmmmountain*. Full instructions on how to teach your child both types of sounds are given on Flashcard 2.

Pure sounds

When teaching your child the Speed sounds it's very important that you don't add an intrusive *uh* to the end of consonant sounds. Try to pronounce them as 'pure' sounds: *m* not *muh*, *f* not *fuh*, *l* not *luh*, etc.

This takes some practice, but if your child learns from you to pronounce the sounds as pure sounds he or she will find it easier later to put the sounds together to make a word. For example, it is easier to put the sounds *c-a-t* together than *cuh-a-tuh* and easier to put the sounds *m-a-n* together than *muh-a-nuh*.

A slight *uh* cannot be helped when saying the sounds *b, d, g, j, w,* and *y*.

Sound-blending

Your child will be ready to blend sounds together to read words once they have learnt the first set of sounds, *m a s d t* and can say them in and out of order at speed.

If your child uses *Read Write Inc. Phonics* at school, he or she may refer to the practice of sounding out letters in words as 'Fred Talk'. Fred is a toy character that some teachers use to engage children in saying the sounds correctly.

The Flashcards set contains ten Instruction cards with fun activities for blending sounds together. Learning to sound-blend can take some time to master, so don't worry if your child doesn't pick it up right away. Carry on teaching your child the next group of Speed sounds. When that group is learnt in and out of order and at speed, practise the sound-blending activities on the Instruction card with those sounds and the previous sounds learnt. Continue until all six sets of sounds have been learnt.

When your child can sound-blend all the groups of Speed sounds, celebrate the success! He or she has reached a major milestone in learning to read.

Using the Storybooks

Read Write Inc. Phonics Storybooks have lively rhyming stories that your child will enjoy reading. To ensure success in reading from the start, the Storybooks also include important activities to prepare your child for reading the words in the stories, plus activities to consolidate what has been read.

It's important that your child follows the six steps to reading success:

⭐ Practise reading the Speed sounds before each story

⭐ Read the Green and Red words before each story

⭐ Read the story

⭐ Re-read the story to reinforce meaning

⭐ Discuss the questions

⭐ Practise reading the Speed words.

After your child completes each of these steps turn to the 'star' page in the Storybook and allow him or her to colour in the achievement stars for that activity. This will motivate your child to carry on learning.

1 Reading the Speed sounds

The Speed sounds for each story are a quick review of the sounds that make up the words in the stories.

Before your child reads each story in the book quickly check that he or she can read the Speed sounds in and out of order and at speed. Practise any which cause uncertainty, until your child can read the whole chart fluently.

Always make sure the sounds are 'pure', without *uh* at the end. (See page 12 of this Handbook.)

When your child has read the Speed sounds let him or her colour in the 'I can read the Speed sounds' star.

2 Reading the Green and Red words

Green words

The Green words are the words in the story that your child will be able to 'go ahead' and sound-blend together as they are made up of the Speed sounds already learnt on the Flashcards.

Your child will be able to read these words in the story much more easily if he or she practises reading them first.

Point to the first word and ask your child to 'sound out' the word first, e.g. *h-a-t* , then blend the sounds together to make the word: *hat*. Continue in this way with all the Green words.

Remember that sometimes one sound is represented by more than one letter, e.g. *th* as in *thin* or *sh* as in *ship*. These are always underlined in the Green words chart to show your child that they have to be pronounced together to make one sound.

If your child gets stuck on a word, ask him or her to 'sound out' the word and then to try and blend the sounds together to say the word. If your child still does not hear the word, say the sounds yourself, quickly.

When your child has read the Green words give plenty of praise and let him or her colour in the 'I can read the Green words' star.

Red words

Learning to read English would be a lot easier if all the words were made up of just the sounds your child has learnt through the Flashcards. Unfortunately, some of the most frequently used and useful words in English have uncommon spellings and don't sound like they look, for example, *said, you* and *the*.

In *Read Write Inc. Phonics* these are called 'Red words'. They are words which can't be read by sound-blending. They have to be learnt by sight.

These words are printed in red in the stories to signal to your child that he or she has to 'stop and think' about how to say them. This support in the first stages of reading helps your child to have early success in reading and ensures that he or she builds up a knowledge bank of useful words.

When your child has read the Red words give plenty of praise and let him or her colour in the 'I can read the Red words' star.

3 Reading the story

Read the Introduction to your child to stimulate interest in the story. Make links to your child's own experiences where possible (and if necessary explain an unfamiliar situation to him or her). Keep it lively and engaging and avoid going off the point. Don't ask your child to read the introduction as they will not have the phonic knowledge to do so.

Your child is now ready to read the story! Don't be tempted to read the story to your child first. If you do, he or she is likely to remember it, and therefore get no real practice in learning to read.

Point to each word, sound-by-sound, for your child and move your finger to the next word when it has been read correctly.

If your child gets stuck on a word encourage sounding out the word and blending the sounds together. If he or she is not able to do this, sound out the word yourself and then ask your child to put the sounds together to make the word. If this does not work, then you say the word. Do be patient with your child. Like learning any new skill it takes practice.

At the bottom of some pages are questions about the story for you to ask your child. In the Level 3 books these appear at the end of the stories. Wait until your child re-reads the story to ask these, when he or she will be able to read the story with greater confidence.

Praise your child's efforts during reading. When the story has been read, encourage your child to colour in the 'I can read the story' star.

4 Re-reading the story

Ask your child to re-read the story. This can be the same day, or the next day. If it is the next day, make sure that he or she reads the Speed sounds, Green words and Red words again.

Re-reading a story helps your child to understand it better. This in turn helps him or her to read the words in the story with more fluency and expression. Your child may be reading in a flat, monotone voice while working out the words. Once the words have been mastered, ask your child to think about how the character is feeling and to try to show expression when reading what that character is saying. Show your child how you would read particular lines.

5 Discussing the questions

When your child is re-reading the story ask him or her the questions that are at the bottom of some of the story pages (or after the story in the Level 3 books). Do not ask your child to read the questions as he or she will not know all the sounds in the words to do so. When your child has re-read the story and you've discussed the questions, let him or her colour in the 'I can answer the questions' star.

6 Reading the Speed words

After each story there is a set of Speed words, which are the main words your child met in the story.

When your child can read the story with ease, encourage him or her to practise reading these individual words as quickly as possible. Read the words across the rows and down the columns and then in and out of order. If there is hesitation or problems with a word encourage your child to sound out the word and then blend the sounds together. Then ask him or her to start again at the beginning of the row or column.

Make this a fun celebration of what your child can do. When he or she can read all the Speed words quickly, without hesitation or error, let your child colour in the 'I can read the Speed words' star. Remember to praise your child's efforts.

Reading the next story

Whether progressing onto the next story in the same book or moving onto a brand new book, ensure you follow the routine of reading the Speed sounds, Green words and Red words first. Then set the scene by reading your child the Introduction to the story.

Ensure your child finishes each story by reading the Speed words. Then finally, and most importantly, always reward your child's efforts with praise.

Reading together

In addition to your child reading the *Read Write Inc. Phonics* Storybooks do read a variety of other books to your child – every bedtime if possible. It is vital to expand his or her vocabulary so, later, when your child reads more advanced books he or she will both read and understand many of the words. Children's literature has a greater source of new and rare words than adults use in everyday conversation, so discuss the meanings of words in the context of the story. What your child can say today he or she will be reading tomorrow.

Join your local library to experience a broad range of authors and genres.

For more information on *Read Write Inc. Phonics* visit the website: www.readwriteinc.com

Synthetic Phonics Glossary

Read Write Inc. and synthetic phonics use vocabulary which may be unfamiliar to many parents. This glossary should familiarise you with some of the terms.

Green words words which your child will be able to read once they have learnt the Speed sounds

Fred Talk saying each sound in a word. See page 13

Pure sounds sounds without an intrusive *uh* at the end, *l* not *luh*, *t* not *tuh*, etc. See page 12

Red words words which do not sound like they look and can't be 'sounded out', e.g. *said, you*. See page 16

Sound-blend blending the sounds in a word together, e.g. *c-a-n* → *can*. This is taught through the activities on the Instructions cards. See page 13

Speed sounds the letters and the sounds that words are made up of. They are taught using the Flashcards and revised before each story. See page 10

Speed words words to be read after the story, that your child should be able to read 'at speed' without the support of the story. See page 19

Synthetic phonics the teaching of reading in which sounds and the letter or letters that represent them are pronounced individually and blended together ('synthesised')

Handwriting

When your child is learning the Speed sounds ensure he or she forms each letter correctly as shown below, always starting where the dot is and following the directional arrows.

m a s d t

i n p g o

c k u b

f e l h sh

r j v y w

th z ch

qu x ng nk